# Songs from Heaven

J. Hoch Lane

**Herd Up Publishing**

Songs from Heaven
Copyright © 2021 by J. Hoch Lane
All Rights Reserved

Published by: Herd Up Publishing
Colorado Springs, CO
HerdUpPublishing@protonmail.com

Any scripture woven into these songs is derived from the King James Version of the Holy Bible. This is the only version of the Word of God the author uses.

ISBN: 978-0-578-33325-0
Library of Congress Control Number: 2021924202

Printed in the United States of America

# − Dedication −

For: The widows, the fatherless, the man of sorrows, the poor, the sick, the brokenhearted, the feebleminded, the captives, the strangers, the brethren, and anyone else searching for hope.

May you find the comfort that only He can give, while His songs are being shared with you.

That's right, dear one. This is for…you.

## – Table of Contents –

| | |
|---|---|
| Praise is Our Escape Route | 1 |
| God's Promises | 2 |
| Hallelujah - You Are Good | 3 |
| We are Redeemed! | 4 |
| Walking on Your Highway | 6 |
| Nothing is Hidden | 7 |
| Morning Star - Arise in Our Hearts | 8 |
| Lord, I Want to Behold Your Face | 9 |
| His Precious Mercy | 10 |
| Born Again | 11 |
| In Returning and Rest... | 12 |
| Open up the Gates! | 13 |
| Lord, Please Continue... | 14 |
| Behold, The Lord | 15 |
| Reign Over Me | 16 |
| Alleluia | 17 |
| I Am | 18 |
| Your Righteousness Revives Me | 19 |
| Renew the Inward Man | 20 |
| Part the Sea | 21 |
| The Job | 22 |
| Your Highness | 24 |
| I'm Standing Here Waiting | 25 |
| Grace is Free | 26 |
| When His Spirit is in It | 27 |
| My Light is Gonna Shine | 28 |
| Strongholds are Falling | 29 |
| The Lord Shall be Unto Thee | 30 |
| Without Holiness | 31 |
| Jesus | 32 |
| Generations | 33 |

| | |
|---|---:|
| Saying What's in My Heart | 34 |
| Our RSVP to Your Invitation | 35 |
| United We Stand | 36 |
| Greater is He that is in Me | 38 |
| When I Grow Up | 40 |
| Predestinated | 41 |
| And You Will Know | 42 |
| Anchor of My Soul | 43 |
| I Am Cleansed | 44 |
| The "Thank You" Cycle | 45 |
| Perfect Love Casts out Fear | 46 |
| Awake Arise | 48 |
| I Want to Know You More | 49 |
| New Heavens and New Earth | 50 |
| One Purchase | 51 |
| I Will Seek You | 52 |
| Your Branches | 54 |
| Yours is the Kingdom | 55 |
| My God Reigneth - (with a timbrel and a dance) | 56 |
| Please Pardon Us | 58 |
| I Will Help Thee | 59 |
| Prayerfully and Carefully | 60 |
| You Are | 61 |
| You Love Me So | 62 |
| Your Wonders Never Cease | 64 |
| Please Pray for Me | 66 |
| Jesus Lives in Us | 68 |
| When I Awake | 69 |
| We're Being Formed | 70 |
| The Truth that You Are | 71 |
| Take Heed, Watch, and Pray | 72 |
| No Other Voices | 73 |
| Common is Rare | 74 |
| Return unto Me | 76 |
| I Do | 77 |
| Let the Tares Grow | 78 |
| I Know You Differently | 79 |

| | |
|---|---|
| Jeremiah | 80 |
| The Mathematician | 82 |
| A Call for Justice | 84 |
| Stephen's Prayer | 86 |
| We Have a Home in You | 87 |

## -Praise is Our Escape Route -

You've given me a million second chances to get it right
Each time I fell, You picked me up and put me beside
Your mighty arm – where I'm safe and I'm sound
Where Your love, mercy, and grace abound

I stepped into Your walls and that's salvation
When I was trapped, I started praisin' You
The gates opened wide – I stepped in, now I'm free
To be who You've called me to be

The prison that held me seemed like forever
Now, I thank You for my heavenly treasure
The Kingdom awaits those who seek Your way out
And praise, praise, praise, praise, praise, praise, praise

And praise is our escape route!

# – God's Promises –

For 25 years, Abraham held on
He was a century old before Isaac came along
He waited and waited and he believed
Which was accounted for righteousness
So, he received – he received

At 84 years old, Anna spent her life
Serving in the temple
She wanted to see Christ
She prayed and she fasted night and day
And when she finally saw Him
Gave thanks right away – right away

God makes good on all His promises
Our job is to simply wait
And He will add far greater than we would give ourselves
But it takes time – time to work it out

Almost 15 years ago, I was told
I married a "family man and a fine fellow"
Every single day I seek God's Kingdom and His will
And now at 40 years of age
That Word's fulfilled – Word's fulfilled

God makes good on all His promises
Our job is to simply wait
And He will add far greater than we would give ourselves
But it takes time – time to work it out

# Hallelujah – You Are Good

Hallelujah – For Your holiness
It's beautiful, peace, joy, and righteousness
You are good
Remember us
Hallelujah – You are good

Forever – Horn of Salvation
You bring forth the gladness of Your nation
You are good
Remember us
Hallelujah – You are good

We rejoice – In Your mighty hands
Who can utter a full acknowledgement of them?
You are good
Remember us
Hallelujah – You are good

## -We are Redeemed! -

Upon the righteous
Upon His sons
Upon the perfect – are the eyes of the Lord

Unto the humble
Unto the meek
Unto all His people – are His ears when we speak

He has redeemed
Our souls from defeat
To inherit His portion
Furnished and free
No longer barren
We're full as can be
I am redeemed! You are redeemed!
Yes, we are Redeemed!

Against the wicked
Against the proud
Against all evil, is the face of our God

Come all ye children
Please gather near
Seek peace and pursue it
And the Good News you'll hear

He has redeemed
Our souls from defeat
To inherit His portion
Furnished and free
No longer barren
We're full as can be
I am redeemed!  You are redeemed!
Yes, we are Redeemed!

# -Walking on Your Highway -

Some people say – It's my way or the highway
Without knowing what they're telling you to choose
Today, I'm gonna take the highway
Because it's Your way
I've got everything to gain and nothing to lose

I make progress when I wait for Your instruction
Before I take a step out on my own
There will be no images molten or graven
The only things: a heart and mind that look like Yours

Please tell me where to go
Please teach me what to say
Please tell me what to do
As I'm walking down Your Highway

> "Son – strive entering in at the strait gate
> Don't be afraid of narrow
> It's so much better than eternal sorrow"

Father – Who can lay anything to the charge of Your elect?
Through Your love for us
We are more than conquerors

Please tell us where to go
Please teach us what to say
Please tell us what to do
As we're walking down Your Highway

# -Nothing is Hidden-

Nothing is hidden
You know all

From the moment I rise up
Until the time I –
Fall down on my knees

Lord, I lift my soul to You
To have me do
As You'd have me to
In the light of Your love

# -Morning Star – Arise in Our Hearts-

Unblamable in holiness
Establish my heart today
Lord, please perfect in my faith
That which is lacking, I pray

Helpers of joy by faith we stand
Not on our own, but in Your hand
Blinded no more by Your light we see
As you manifest Your mysteries

Morning Star – Arise in our hearts
Shine through the dark and lead us

Morning Star – Arise in our hearts
We lift our hands; Lord, bring us

# -Lord, I Want to Behold Your Face -

Lord, I want to behold Your face
In righteousness, You are my stay
Casting them down and delivering my soul
From the wicked – with Thy sword
Lord, that's grace

Lord, I want to behold Your Face

## - His Precious Mercy -

I bless You, Lord
I praise You
I rejoice in You, Lord
I thank You

Thank You for Your mercy

Mercy enables me to be holy
It gives me a second chance
To be transformed into Your image, Lord
And I thank You in advance
Because although I don't yet look like You
You've promised if I keep Your way
That I'll obtain Your world from above
I'll tell this earthly world –

"I won't conform to your ways
And I refuse to be condemned with you
The Lord is renewing my mind
And I won't take His precious mercy for granted
Because a greater gift no one can find."

# Born Again

Our lives are hidden in You
We want to put on the man that is new
We pray these old deeds are put to death
And we see through Your bond of perfectness

We want Your peace to rule in our hearts
Today and forever, Lord – we're thankful
Whatsoever we do in Your name
It's by Jesus Christ whom we proclaim

Kindness comes before – salvation
Washing and renewal – regeneration
Clothed in white we remain
It is by Your Spirit we're born again

## -In Returning and Rest...-

Glory to God
Glory to God

Waiting on You doesn't make me helpless
It means I accept that You can do it better
You've got a plan for all of this
Thank You for Your righteous judgments

In returning and rest
Quietness
Confidence
... My strength is You

Glory to God
Glory to God

Suffering for You doesn't mean it's hopeless
It means that I want to obey Your precepts
No longer only servitude
Now a forever friendship

In returning and rest
Quietness
Confidence
... I'm safe in You

# -Open up the Gates!-

This is the voice of rejoicing
Open up the gates
Your mercy endures forever
So, forever I'll give You praise

Mighty and valiant are Your works, O Lord
Your right hand lifted high
I'll praise You for You've heard me
I will live and shall not die

I will live and shall not die

## -Lord, Please Continue...-

I want to be purified
I want to be new
I want to be changed, Lord
Please continue –
To do a work in my life
To do a work in my heart
So that we will never be apart

As You Are
I want to see You
I want to know You
Please continue –
To do a work in my life
To do a work in my heart
So that we will never be apart

Every step that I take
May it be for You
I want to walk in love
Please continue –
To do a work in my life
To do a work in my heart
So that we will never be apart

# – Behold, The Lord –

Behold, the Lord
And He has our reward
Nothing He is shall wither
Nothing He does shall fade
He promised we'd live forever, and today's the day
Today's the day!

> *"Behold, I Am the Lord*
> *And I have your reward*
> *I will open rivers in dry lands*
> *I will make the desert blossom by My hands*
> *I've promised you restoration*
> *And today's the day*
> *Today's the day – Behold."*

# -Reign Over Me-

You are the light among the darkness
You are the white when all around me is scarlet
You are the voice when everything is silent

Reign over me

You are my friend not only my master
You are the calm in the midst of disaster
You are the constant when nothing else has lasted

Reign over me

You are the Lord who graciously teaches
When it's out of arm's length –
You're the One who reaches
You have provided everything that I've needed

Reign over me

## -Alleluia-

You are worthy, O Lord
To receive glory, honor, and power
For You've created all
And they're here for Your pleasure
Alleluia, Alleluia, Alleluia, Alleluia

We give You thanks, O Lord
Who Was, and Is, and Is coming
Because You've taken to Yourself
Your great power, and reigned in glory
Alleluia, Alleluia, Alleluia, Alleluia

## -I Am-

*"As the snow and rain come down from Heaven to water the earth
So will My Words be that come forth from out of My mouth*

*The hills and the mountains break forth and they'll sing
There will be gladness
There will be clapping from the trees*

*I Am your shelter
I Am your hiding place in the wind
I Am your shadow
I Am your river in a weary land*

*I Am exalted – For I dwell on high
Wisdom and knowledge – the stability of your times*

*I will regard your prayer when you call upon My Name
I will wipe away all of your tears
I'll wipe away all of your shame*

*Wait upon Me
My promises are near
You will receive them
You will see, know, you will hear."*

# -Your Righteousness Revives Me -

You are the Bread of Life
You feed me spiritually
I'll never hunger again
You're faithful to commune with me

So grateful for Your blood at the Cross
No longer in captivity
I'm worthy to suffer for You
Your Spirit is here to comfort me

You took on the body of flesh
To overcome the death that was waiting
You help me when I am weary
Your righteousness revives me

Hallelujah
Praise You, Lord
I'm hopeful You will remember me for good

Hallelujah
Salvation guaranteed
I praise You, Lord, for… for everything

## —Renew the Inward Man—

Renew the inward man inside of me
Day by day it's needed
Some say strength
Some say money
But it's love that makes us mighty
Mighty, Lord, in You

One man plants
One man waters
Both have different callings
But both are called by You
They are equally precious
No reason to be jealous
The increase comes from You

A many membered body
Many parts are needed
They all are in God's army
And they are marching
Fashioned to Your will

One flock
Many sheep are scattered
Who now are being gathered
Gathered unto You

## -Part the Sea -

Many years ago
Many years ago You called me
Called me to stand by the sea
And as I'm still standing here
I cry out to You, Lord
Lord, when will You part the sea for me?

And You say,

> *"Move forward.*
> *This next step is up to you.*
> *I have done My part, but your part is step two.*
> *When will you trust Me –*
> *Trust Me through and through?*
> *I will part the sea*
> *When your feet start to move."*

## -The Job-

Hi, I'm here to apply for the job posting
I'm sure there are several questions you'll be asking me
Let me ask first if I may
About the job – about the pay
Who will I be working for
And is this a job He's done before?

Our Leader is someone who first learned how to serve
He's already given far more than we deserve
He is patient – He is kind
And He'll be with you all the time
His name's Jesus – He's suffered all
When you have a problem that's Who you'll call
He's great with mercy – He forgives
Long suffers so that you will live
As far as wage He pays top price
After all He did lay down His life

Tell me – are you interested?
There are still many applicants…

Yes! Sure thing! Absolutely!
What He says goes!
I want Him to control me from my head down to my toes
I'm able and my answer's plain
Nothing to lose and all to gain
I'm willing to work overtime – to be a part of His design

Yes! Sure thing! Absolutely!
What He says goes!
I want Him to control me from my head down to my toes
I can start right away
I'm gonna cancel all my plans today
I just know that I'll succeed –
and I thank Him for accepting me!

# -Your Highness-

Let the thoughts of Your heart and Your mind
Be my only motivation
You oversee my soul
And my whole life has been preparation

We rejoice, O Lord, in Your highness
Abounding in Your work
Your rest is glorious
Your anointing is what lifts the yoke

Your Kingdom is in Your great power
Let Your Name forever be magnified
You are the Judge of all
Every word will be verified

*"I reward those who diligently seek Me*
*Entirely blameless I'm preserving thee*
*I Am the Author and Finisher of faith*
*And when I'm done, you won't depart from Me*

*You're perfected with one single offering*
*By the One unashamed to call you friend*
*According to My foreknowledge*
*I Am your Father, the beginning, and the end"*

# -I'm Standing Here Waiting-

My heart cries out to You
I am trying to give it all to You
There's a war that is raging inside my soul
O Lord, please make me whole

I know that You're perfecting my spirit
And I know that with You there are no limits
But I see myself stumbling, so I'm discouraged
O Lord, I pray for endurance

My hope, O Lord, is in You
As Your faithfulness is always new
So, I'm standing here and I'm waiting
For Your mercy, thank God, that is unfailing

And I praise Your Holy Name
It's not by my works, it's by Your grace
If I really, truly, completely believe it
Why am I still trying to achieve it?

My hope, O Lord, is in You
As Your faithfulness is always new
So, I'm standing here and I'm waiting
For Your mercy, thank God, that is unfailing

# -Grace is Free-

Grace is free
It's a gift to you and me
Not just in this place, but in this hour
We find life
When we know we're justified
You've already paid the price, by Your power

There's a reason You'll take me as I am
Because the precious blood of the Lamb
Gave me the chance to choose to be like You

So, whatever is in me
That doesn't bend my knee
Making it simple to walk away easily
I beg You –

Lord, burn it up, and tear it down
Until all of me is on the ground
Yielding…

To Your perfect will
I need You still

Lord, burn it up, and tear it down
Until all of me is on the ground
Yielding…

To Your perfect will
I need You still
I need You still

# When His Spirit is in It

When His Spirit is in it
You're gonna win it
Beauty for ashes
Gladness for grief
It's a beautiful trade off
Because He's making us
Perfect, entire, wanting nothing – complete

Joy comes in the morning
We're changed glory to glory
He'll make a way
Hope says I'm not ashamed
So, I'll keep my head held high
Eyes pointed to the sky
Humbly expecting to be His bride

# -My Light is Gonna Shine-

I thought I needed to start by changing the lightbulb
I didn't know it wasn't broken until You turned it on
Darkness is gone, and only the Light belongs

So, my light is gonna shine
I won't be afraid this time
When You tell me to speak
I'll know You're holding onto me

You've never ever given up
Though I thought I wasn't good enough
I don't want to run and hide
I want You to dwell on the inside

It's hard not to feel guilty among accusations
And I see that I believed them until You set me free
Fullness dwells in You
Because in You lies every truth

So, my light is gonna shine
I won't be afraid this time
When You tell me to speak
I'll know You're holding onto me

You've never ever given up
Though I thought I wasn't good enough
I don't want to run and hide
I want You to dwell on the inside

# -Strongholds are Falling-

How can I be anything but grateful
When I receive the correction that I've been praying for?
Nations will see Your judgment
As You fulfill the work of faith
It's the perfect kind of love
When Your truth is spoken of

Strongholds are falling
But You're still holding me strong
They've been imposing and I just want them gone
I need the spirit of my mind renewed
Your opinion is all that I need
So, please continue to speak Your truth in love
Cause that's what sets me free

How can I be anything but humble
Once I've tasted of Your Holy presence?
Patience and faith are manifest tokens
As they inherit Your promises
It's the perfect kind of love
When Your truth is spoken of

Strongholds are falling
But You're still holding me strong
They've been imposing and I just want them gone
I need the spirit of my mind renewed
Your opinion is all that I need
So, please continue to speak Your truth in love
Cause that's what sets me free

## -The Lord Shall be unto Thee -

Violence shall no more be heard in thy land
Wasting nor destruction within thy borders
But thou shalt call thy walls "Salvation"
And thy gates "Praise"
The sun shall be no more thy light by day
Neither for brightness shall the moon give light
But the Lord shall be unto thee
But the Lord shall be unto thee
Yes the Lord shall be unto thee
An everlasting Light and Glory

Because we have:

Boldness and access with confidence by the grace of Him
We confess Jesus Christ

He saved us and delivered us
He overcame death for all of us
We're headed for Paradise

We are the children of God
Because we belong to Jesus
And since He belongs to You, Lord,
We too are Yours

# Without Holiness

Without holiness I won't see You
Please deal with me as Your son
I will make mention of Your name, Lord
I will praise You from the earth
You uphold all by the Word of Your power
Jesus purged all sin by His blood

## – Jesus –

Endure and live and abide forever
Christ, You are incorruptible seed
Disallowed of men – indeed rejected
Yet so very precious to me
You love and in turn are reviled
They've questioned Your every step
Suffering wrongfully while patient
And obedient unto death

Still I choose to follow You
For You are risen
And as Your co-heir, I too am chosen
A door will be opened
Where we won't be hurting
As Your peculiar people – diligently learning

Into Your reality
We will see clearly
There'll be no more suffering
For we'll be free
No longer rejected
We'll be accepted
No longer misunderstood – royal priesthood

A chosen generation
Accepting Christ as salvation
We'll have the answers
Blessed beyond words
We are not all alone
We'll be seated at Your throne
Living to serve You – Jesus is Lord!

## -Generations-

I'm not only Your daughter
I'm the daughter of Your daughter
You are just as much her Father as mine

I'm not only Your daughter
I'm the mother of Your daughter
We have the same living water and blood

Your relationship with nations
Covers multiple generations
Across all of Your locations at once

We're a grateful congregation
Jesus lived and died for our salvation
No greater loving demonstration will be found

We accept this invitation
As part of Your predestination
It's a joyous celebration for us all

## - Saying What's in My Heart -

All my life I've been encouraged
To speak what's on my mind
And all my life I've been discouraged
From saying what's in my heart

But why would I want to speak what is on my mind
Instead of in my heart
When that is where You are?

Cultivated like a garden
To improve the growth of – The Fruit of the Spirit:
Joy, peace, long-suffering, and love,
Gentleness, goodness, faith, temperance, and meekness
Walking in the Spirit – I won't fulfill the lusts of my flesh

And why would I want to see what the world will see
When it all fades away, but only You remain?

No you can't serve God and mammon
Only one can occupy the throne
I choose wisdom over wealth
Lord, don't let me stand here on my own

No you can't have two masters
Double-minded men unstable in all their ways
Tossed to and fro with every wind
Lord, help me stand firm in this place

## – Our RSVP to Your Invitation –

You Are our Advocate and Sacrifice
You pray for us, and You paid the price
Glory to God we know we're justified
Fellowship restored through Jesus Christ

Obedience is how we're purified
No longer afraid to come to the Light
Here we are, Lord, we don't want to hide
We want You to dwell inside

# United We Stand

There's one Lord over all
And Christ is all in all
When we call on His name, we are no different
So, Jew or Greek, bond or free, he or she
We're all the same
And instead of finding reasons why we should be divided
Let's stand in love and be united

He is rich unto all who call upon His name
He gives Himself freely to everyone
So, walk or crawl, short or tall, big or small
We're all the same
And instead of finding reasons why we should be divided
Let's stand in love and be united

With one heartbeat
There is no defeat
When we obey His commands
In victory we stand

We're the same
In His Holy Name

And though we're called to be separated
Our duty has always been to love
There is no room for opinions or hatred
We're all saved by the same blood

So, black or white, blind or sight, weak or might
We're all the same
And instead of finding reasons why we should be divided
Let's stand in love and be united

# -Greater is He that is in Me -

You are my Defender
You are my strength
Your mercy has no measure
Your wisdom has no length

You hear, You forgive, You do, You heal

Greater is He that is in me
Glory to God, Glory
Glory to God, Glory

You are my Counselor
You are my Friend
You are forever
Your love has no end

You hear, You forgive, You do, You heal

Greater is He that is in me
Glory to God – glory
Glory to God – glory

You are our Shepherd
We are Your sheep
You lay us on Your shoulders
Comforting while we weep

We cry, we believe, we change, we're healed

Greater is He
Greater is He
Greater is He – that is in me

## When I Grow Up

When I grow up I want to become child like
Absolutely completely trusting You
So, when You tell me to "Let go"
I'm not afraid of what's below
I'll know You're in control as my Father
I'm learning to be – Your daughter

When I grow up I want to be Your planting
Watered by the river of the Lord
Deeply rooted in an earth – where righteousness
    dwells with new birth
There's nowhere else I'd rather be –
    than on Your mountain
Refreshed by Your life-giving fountain

When I grow up I want to hunt treasure
Not the kind that is buried by the sea
I'll only need Your guiding light
And that still small voice inside
I'll find my prosperity inside eternity
You've been storing it there for me

## -Predestinated-

Your will
Your will
I choose to be in Your will
Sever the wicked from me
Destroy them with the breath of Your lips
Until Your voice is all I believe

I want to let go
Of all these things that I hold
Nothing completes me but You
Destroy them with the brightness of Your coming
Every Word that You speak, Lord, is truth

All I need to know is that You're in control
You hold the whole world in Your hand
I give my doubt and weakness –
And I trade them for Jesus
Predestinated for Your Holy Land

I give my doubt and weakness –
And I trade them for Jesus
Predestinated for Your Holy land

# -And You Will Know-

I've been so disappointed
Like I've let everyone down
Wishing I could help more
Responsible and bound

But then I realized they would thank me
Instead of praising You
You bring the salvation
And the Spirit of Truth

And they will know
You are the Lord
And they will know You are the Lord

There's a witness – I can feel Him
He's a rushing mighty wind
Flowing all around me
His warm embrace is on my skin

And there's a witness – I can feel Him
He's burning deep within
He's abiding in me
And soon I'll abide with Him

*"And you will know*
*I Am the Lord*
*And you will know I Am the Lord"*

# Anchor of My Soul

There's a heaviness
Pulling on me like a chain
I don't know if I can even face the day
I feel forsaken and afraid

What would it be like
To have someone understand my life
Someone who could see me as I really am
Then, Jesus spoke and said, "I can"

These sufferings, though vast
Can't compare to what will come at last
Consolation comes from the Holy One
When He appears and calls me, "Son"

Purify my heart
So, I behold glory where You are
Although I have very little strength
Yet, I rejoice in Your name

Anchor of my soul
Sure and steadfast is my hope
Tethered to the throne of the Great I Am
The way first taken by the Lamb

Holy Holy Holy Holy
Nothing sacred falls
Nothing sacred falls
Lord, please raise these ruins –
And dwell here once and for all

## - I Am Cleansed -

I am forgiven
I am redeemed
I've been adopted – and it's better than it seems

You see, I have a Father
And He has set me free
As far as any other – They no longer have a hold on me

I am looking for You, Jesus
Your blood was given for my purchase
I owe my whole life to You
This gift won't be wasted
Guilty all of my days, but Your great mercy I've tasted

I am… cleansed

Your ways are higher
Your instruction is greater
Your love has no equal
You're the faithful Creator
Your existence is endless
So are Your mercies and graces
Promises now performance
Every man will sing praises

I am begotten again
Faith unto salvation
Jesus rose from the dead
Bringing hope to all nations

I am… regenerated

# – The "Thank You" Cycle –

Every time You meet a need of mine – I thank You
So, Thank You
And every time I thank You – You meet another need

But this time I just can't stop praising You
This cycle won't end of me thanking You

Because every need that I have is met
Every need that I have is met
I don't need above, beyond, or too much
All I need, All I need – is enough

Your way of righteousness is for me
Your way of righteousness is for me
I don't need to wander, to flee, or to stray
All I need, All I need – Is Your way

You answer everything for me, O Lord
You answer everything for me, O Lord
I don't need what I think or what the world wants me
    to learn
All I need, All I need – is Your Word

I delight in pleasing only You, my King
I delight in pleasing only You, my King
I don't need precious gems, or great wealth to pursue
All I need, All I need – Is You

## -Perfect Love Casts out Fear-

Here I am
Waiting for Your Words of life
Expecting something great to come and ease my mind
But the silence is so loud – it's really all that I hear
I'm waiting for that still small voice to remind me that You're near
But it's not Your Voice that's missin'
There's fear in these afflictions

Perfect love – casts out fear
And if there's one thing that I know
It's that You love perfectly
There's nothing to be afraid of
I'm gonna let go and trust You –
And overcome myself

Here I am
Staring at these hardworking hands
They're telling me it's all for nought with nothing to show for them
But they're filled with the unseen things – It is not emptiness
Oppression is far and terror hides itself when I'm established in righteousness
This labor hasn't been in vain
Your Word always remains

Perfect love – casts out fear
And if there's one thing that I know
It's that You love perfectly
There's nothing to be afraid of
I'm gonna let go and trust You –
And overcome myself
And overcome myself

# -Awake Arise -

Awake
Awake
It's time to awake
The Lord sustains
It's time to be brave
Be of good courage and don't be dismayed
Awake
Awake
Lord, You're the only way

Arise
Arise
It's time to arise
The Father gives life
It's time to realize
Be of good comfort – your faith makes you whole
Arise
Arise
Lord, You're our only hope

Help me, Lord
Help me, my God

*"Awake*
*Arise*
*Put on the Armor of Light"*

# – I Want to Know You More –

Try my heart
Until it's pure and beautiful
I want to know You more and more and more
Lord, I want to know You more

The hills all bow
And the earth, it trembles
I want to fear You more and more and more
I want to fear You more

I want to be slow to anger
I want to be swift to hear
I want to be silent in Your presence, Lord
And slow to speak my own words, Lord

What You give to me, Lord
I gather and return unto You
I want to serve You more and more and more
I want to serve You more

Will You try my heart
Until it's pure and beautiful?
I want to know You more and more and more and more…

# -New Heavens and New Earth -

My heart burns within me
As Your words come to life
And I am unashamed when I wait on You
The entrance has been provided – Your Kingdom is at hand
Take my heart, take my soul – To Your Holy land

All tears will be wiped away
There shall be no more death
Former things shall pass away
Sorrow, crying, and pain
For You will dwell with us and we shall be with You
We're Your people, You're our God – Faithful and True

You make all things new, Lord
New heavens and new earth
Wherein dwells righteousness – available by our new birth
You're the Alpha and Omega
You give to all who thirst
Carry us away, we will be saved – to the uttermost

And we look forward to the coming of the Day of the Lord
The heavens being on fire shall be dissolved
The Day of the Lord comes as a thief in the night
Tell me, what manner of persons ought we be?
The longsuffering of the Lord is our salvation
Be diligent that we'll be found of Him in peace
And we'll look forward to the new heavens and new earth
Afterall, it's what He's promised you and me

# -One Purchase -

There's only one purchase worth purchasing
And over my life, I've bought everything
But I would trade it all for the chance to be
Forever with my King

None of it matters
It's vanity
I'll get this off my chest
And lay it at Your feet

Jesus paid the price for me at Calvary
When He died for me

So, here's my offering
It's not much but it's everything

Lord, there's nothing You can't do
There's nothing too hard for You

And I offer thanksgiving and give You my praise
In front of these people – I am unashamed

## – I Will Seek You –

I will seek You in the morning
I will seek Your Kingdom first
Don't let me wander away out of Your presence
Don't let me be out of Your care
But keep me in Your hands, O God
To where even a fool cannot err

I'm trusting You to make my steps perfect
I'm asking You to direct my ways
Don't let me wander away
Don't let me stray
But keep me – where I'll dwell safely

I'm scared
And I fear
But Lord, my fear of You
Is what will get me through

Will you take this burden off of me
And replace it with You alone?
I need to be freed by Your anointing
I need to hear only Your Voice
Won't you take this yoke from off my neck?
For You are my choice

Our bond is all that matters
Your Word is all I seek
Don't let me throw it away
I ask You today
Will You seek me while I'm seeking You?

I'm scared
And I fear
But Lord, my fear of You
Is what will get me through

## -Your Branches-

What started off as a tiny seed
Has grown into a mighty tree
Where the birds of the air – and even we
Find shelter among Your branches

No longer saplings on our own
Grafted into Your vine, Lord, we have grown
It's a comfort to know that we're not alone
Yes, You are the Head of this home

You are our Father
The Lord of Lords
We are Your children
Yes, we are Yours

# -Yours is the Kingdom -

For Yours is the Kingdom
What's that in Your hand?
Power and might
And strength to make us stand

I offer my heart – willingly
Everything You give me, Lord
Already came from Thee

# –My God Reigneth–
## (with a timbrel and a dance)

This is a new song
The Lord has held His peace so long
He's refrained, but He'll repay

This is a new song
The Lord has held His peace so long
He's been still, but now He will –

Destroy and devour
Vengeance is my God's
He will prevail against His enemies at once

My God reigneth
My God reigneth

He's called me in righteousness
He's holding my hand in His
To open the eyes of the blind
To bring out the prisoners from the dark side

My God reigneth
My God reigneth

His throne is established
He is everlasting

Inhabitants of the rock
Are shoutin' from the mountain tops

"Glory and praise we declare unto You today"
"Glory and praise we declare unto You today"

"Thy God reigneth – Behold your God!"

# – Please Pardon Us –

You are good, Lord
Please pardon us as we seek You
We're preparing our hearts
In order to finally greet You

Hear us and heal us
We're Your children and You love us
You are good, Lord
Please pardon us as we seek You

Purify us through these trials, Lord
We desire to do Your will
White as snow – these crimson sins will become as wool

Hear us and heal us
We're Your children and You love us
You are good, Lord
Please pardon us as we seek You

# - I Will Help Thee -

Holding my right hand
He says unto me,

*"Fear not – I will help thee*
*I will strengthen you*
*I will uphold you*
*And I will help you everyday*
*Fear not"*

## -Prayerfully and Carefully -

Holy King and mighty King
I come to You in everything
Oh, prayerfully and carefully – I stand in awe of You

Substitutionary sacrifice
The blood of Christ
Fountain of life
Oh snares of death – they have conquered you

Our place of refuge is in the truth

## - You Are -

You are the words I speak
You are the songs I sing
You are everything to me

You are the good in me
You are what sets me free
You are everything to me

And I just want to praise You
And I just want to worship You
And I lift Your Name on high
For You are my God

## -You Love Me So-

You tell me to endure
And it sounds so sweet and wonderful
Until the true meaning is pure
Then I realize I've been leaning on my own understanding
And You're –
Telling me to bear this patiently

And oh
You tell me this because You love me so
And You want me to know
It's the only way to grow

And I trust You

As Judge, Lawgiver, and King
You maintain my cause and cover me in absolutely everything
And I realize it has everything to do with You and nothing with me

My only job is to obey

And oh
You tell me this because You love me so
And You want to protect me where I go
But it'll be by Your way and not my own

And I trust You
I trust You
I praise You and I worship You
I need You, Lord – in every way
I need You, Father – every day

## -Your Wonders Never Cease -

Praises
I can't stop singing Your praises
I'm thankful for Your greatness –
Power, glory, victory, and majesty

Wonders
I've started a list of Your wonders
I must admit – there's too much to cover
Your wonders never cease

Here's what You've done for me:

>You removed me from an evil town
>You rescued me from death
>You're with me throughout this journey and
>   at the end I know You're what's left
>
>You've done a work in my family
>You've prepared a place of rest
>I can't begin to thank You, Lord, for always
>   doing what's best
>
>You're working out my salvation

Many times You've restored my soul
You haven't forgotten my marriage
O Lord, You're making me whole
You've given me a way to worship You
You've given me a life
You became my ever-faithful friend
    delivering me from inside

You fight for me in my afflictions
You cover me in Your love
You've given me something to hope for
    and if that still wasn't enough…

You sent Your Son to die for me
You've forgiven all of my sins
You promised me a room inside Your house of
    many mansions

In Your grasp
My life has always been in Your grasp
Fully satisfied I am in knowing that –
I'm held by the King of Kings

Thank You for all You've done for me!

## −Please Pray for Me −

Humbly on my knees, Lord, I come to You
Intercede – Prince of Peace – like only You can do
There's an urgency that I've never felt before
So, I'm asking You, O Lord

Please pray for me
You're the only chance I have, Lord
Please pray for me
And I thank You in advance, Lord
I believe You hear my prayer
Please pray for me

Humbly on my knees, Lord, I come to You
Comfort me – Father of mercies like only You can do
There's an urgency that I've never felt before
So, I'm asking You, O Lord

Please deliver me
You're the only chance I have, Lord
Please deliver me
And I thank You in advance, Lord
I believe You hear my prayer
Please deliver me

You're in the midst of two or three – who gather in
    Your name
Unbelief can't stop or change You, Lord
Forever You're the same

I honor You
I give You praise
I worship Your name – Ancient of Days
I honor You
I give You praise
I worship Your name – Ancient of Days

I believe You hear my prayer
I believe You're everywhere
I believe You hear my prayer – Amen

# – Jesus Lives in Us –

Some people don't know
You care for their soul – but we do
And You've placed that same care in our hearts
So that You have people You can use

So, I lift up the fatherless, the poor, the afraid
The widows and those –
Who call on Your Name

These needs are much too big for me
But they're just the right size for You

How do you do –
Those miracles that feed multitudes?
With a couple fish and a few loaves of bread
That hungry crowd left full instead!
And only You can fill them up
But now Jesus lives in us
Jesus lives in us

Help us understand
That this impossible task is possible
When we put it back in Your hands

Help us – through prayer
Gather up the sorrowful – and put them in Your care

## -When I Awake-

When I awake
I'll be in Your likeness

When I awake
I'll be satisfied

When I awake
This burial will be over
And I will behold Your face

## -We're Being Formed -

There are parts of me that have been maimed in this life
There are spots
There are stains
There are blemishes

But You're doing a work
Yes, You're cleaning me up
You're refining me
So that I'm not temporary

You're making me permanent
Somebody that You can use over and over and over
I owe my life to You
If two thirds are cut off from me
The remaining third will do
For the purpose You've chosen for me
What's purified will worship You

Perfect soundness comes from You
The times of refreshing –
And restitution too
We weren't just created
We weren't simply born

We're being made
We're being formed

## -The Truth that You Are -

We are beautiful
When Your beauty is upon us, Lord
And we are merciful when
Filled with Your mercies – we are

The unstable can't be called faithful
But You, Lord, are steady as a rock

Beautiful, merciful, faithful – God You are

You are wonderful
Because You are filled with wonder, Lord
And You're all-powerful
Because all power is Yours

The respecter of persons can't be called fair
But You show no partiality

Wonderful, powerful, just – Lord You are…

Beautiful, merciful, faithful, wonderful, powerful, just –
Lord, we acknowledge You for the truth that You are

# -Take Heed, Watch, and Pray -

More of You, Lord
Less of me
I want more of You
I want less of me

Father, I thank You for giving us one Word
Before we even have to face the dangers of this world
And even though instruction – it differs every one
There are things that are written that apply to everyone:
> *"Take heed, watch, and pray!"*

That's great instruction for everyday
Cause we just never know
What is waiting for us down the road

Father, I thank You for hearing our prayers
Before we even have the chance to go out anywhere
And even though the lives we live look different every one
There's one direction we're told to walk that pertains to everyone:
> *"Walk lowly, bowed down."*

We're perfect when humility is found
No yeast - flat on the ground
Unleavened bread is safe and sound

More of You, Lord
Less of me
I want more of You
I want less of me

## -No Other Voices -

Your promises keep me strong
While these troubles keep raging on
But the battle is already won. . .

Lord, I wanna hear Your Voice – and no other voices

Lord, I wanna hear Your Voice – no other voices

Lord, I wanna hear Your Voice – no other voices

Lord, I wanna hear Your Voice – no other voices

Lord, I wanna hear Your Voice – and no other voices

## Common is Rare

My favorite color's yellow
My favorite season's fall
I used to not like Mondays –
Now I don't mind them at all

You don't have to be like me
And I won't be like you
But reachin' for the higher goal – is what we need to do

One heart
One mind
Striving together for a faith one of its kind
One Lord
One hope of our calling
One body
One Father
One God

What does it mean to have all things common?
With one head – We're complete in Christ
Ministering of our substance –
Means everything's provided in this life
With one soul we're lacking nothing
No we don't need a thing
Cause with Jesus there's One Spirit, One Baptism,
    One King of Kings

What does it take to have all things common?
It takes a willingness to share
And if I've learned one thing about the word "common"
It's that having things in common
Is really, really common…
But having all things common – is rare

## – Return unto Me –

Every day, I'm standing at a crossroad
One way points to the left
And the other points to the right
But I can't just stand here
I must keep moving –
Until one way's right in front of me
And the other way's behind

The wide road is level – but it's darker
The narrow road is rocky – but there's light
Two voices beckon me
But I choose to follow
The One that speaks softly but with might:

*"Return unto Me means –
your focus is entirely on what I have to say
Return unto Me means
you are merciful in helping others that you meet along the way
Return unto Me means
you prioritize listening and you obey*

*You're facing Me only
your back is turned to every other way
Return unto Me – today*

*There's only one destination
Where you'll be safely in My hands.*

*Return unto Me – and stand."*

## – I Do –

Dearly Beloved,
We're gathered here today
To join this people –
To the God who'll always reign

He's loved us and cherished us
In sickness and in health
We will honor Him
Above all else

Outwardly and inwardly – willingly we bow
Kneeling before Him, we, renew these wedding vows

I do, Lord
I do, Lord
We gladly say, "I do"

As wives obey their husbands, we, give reverence
    unto You

## －Let the Tares Grow －

If I try to explain the things which can't be seen
It unnecessarily drives a wedge in between
Yesterday I said, "Oh no! What can I do?"
But today I say, "Dear Lord, I've got a problem for you!"

It's all about Your timeline and not my own
And I trust when You're ready – You'll make these things known
I don't have to figure out
How, when, where, or why…
I just know I'm not The Fixer, so I won't even try

If I don't have fear – then I have a sound mind
Self-discipline puts that fear –
Puts that fear behind!
Now I finally understand the power of prayer
It really does rid me – of these worldly cares

My intentions have always been good and with love
This divine wisdom correcting me first came from above
It's not about my hopes, my dreams, or my will…
I just know I love you, brethren –
And I always will!

So, I'll let the tares grow and encourage the wheat
These tares are between you and God
They've got nothin' to do with me
And I'll only mention them as I pray –

"Lord, have it Your way.
Have it Your way."

# -I Know You Differently-

Father, I live unto You
Jesus, I live through You
Holy Spirit, I live with You

You're all the same
But I know You differently

Father, my life is unto You because You gave it to me
Jesus, my life's through You because Your blood set me free
Holy Spirit, my life's with You cause You're always with me
For in You, Lord, I live, and I move, and have my being

Because You are available to everyone
We can all have a personal one on one
Godhead, You are absolute Divinity
I'm so grateful that You've chosen us to be Your offspring

Father, unto You – I must yield
Jesus, through You – I can yield
Holy Spirit, with You – I will yield

You're all the same
But I know You differently

# – Jeremiah –

Jeremiah had already been – struck and imprisoned
Told not to speak a word
Because the people disliked what they'd heard

When Jeremiah's friends came near
Said, "From you the Lord will hear.
Go to Him today, and see what He has to say."
Jeremiah said willingly,
"Behold, I have heard your plea
And it shall come to pass – He will answer all that you ask."

Then they said,
"Bad or good – we'll obey the Voice of the Lord
That it may be well with us
True and faithful the Lord we trust."

After 10 days – The Lord's Word came
Jeremiah gathered them to proclaim,

> *"If you abide in this land, I will build you with My hand.*
> *But if you say "no," and off to Egypt you go –*
> *the sword that you have feared – will overtake you there."*

Jeremiah faithfully –
Warned of captivity, famine, and pestilence
And to cease from their own confidence

Then those proud men said,
"Someone brainwashed your head!
That didn't come from the Lord!"
And they disobeyed every word…

They accepted him no more
Committing great evil against their soul
Told him they stopped listening
Because the prophecy was displeasing

The Lord could no longer bear
All the rebellion there
He said,
> *"We'll see whose word stands –*
> *During a visitation to the land."*

His anger would've relented
If only they would've repented
Acknowledged He's always right
And thanked Him for the warnings in their life

What was first received as a threat,
Was intended as a gift
Believe what He's telling you
And allow His truth to let you live!

Blessed is he who comes in the name of the Lord!
Blessed is he who comes in the name of the Lord!
Blessed is he who comes in the name of the Lord!

## -The Mathematician -

Jesus
He's the one who teaches us
About His Spirit and what it means to love
I have some examples
To explain this revelation
That He's more than a teacher –
He's a mathematician

Length of days, all things, and to your faith He adds virtue
Grace and peace, love, and mercy He multiplies unto you
Now I don't know if He subtracts, but your sins He takes away
Then He divides the light from darkness and the night from the day

He adds
He multiplies
He takes away
And He divides

He adds
He multiplies
He takes away
And He divides

So, you see – there's so much more than what you may
 have initially thought…
Written scripture isn't all that Jesus taught – Jesus taught

He's involved in your life
And He wants the best for you
So, He'll add learning to your lips
And take away branches that bear no fruit

# – A Call for Justice –

I am calling for Your justice
I'm pleading for Your truth
I know You go before me
And I want to follow You

Father, help me remember
Lest I forget
It doesn't help me when I worry
It only causes harm when I fret

These times, these times –
Are to help me trust You more, that all these fears depart
And these trials, these precious trials –
Are to humble me and to know what's in my heart

Lord, I'm calling for Your justice
I'm pleading for Your truth
I'm not interested in listening
To anything that's not from You

Father, help me remember
Everything You've done
I've got a giant standing in front of me
But I will not be undone

You said, You said –

*"Every tribe walk down and grab one stone from the riverbed.
These stones, these river stones – are one and the same that
sent Goliath to the grave."*

Lord, I'm calling for Your justice
I'm pleading for Your truth
I know that You've confirmed me
And, I will always look to You

## Stephen's Prayer

When Stephen cried – "Lord, lay not this sin to their charge!"
I often think that I
Would fail, it'd be too hard
I must confess – if that were me, I'd be resenting
If to my death, people just stood there consenting

But Stephen's prayer –
To forgive that specific iniquity
Gave Saul the chance
To become Paul eventually
I pray to forgive, if that were ever to happen to me
I would want the "Sauls" to live
Bearing Your Name to anyone listening

Set my mind – on the things that be of You
That I deny myself
Take up my cross and follow You
If I lose my life, for the Gospel's sake it's true
That I will ever live
Because my soul will be safe with You

# -We Have a Home in You-

Glory and honor are in His presence
Strength and gladness are in His place
Save us, gather us, deliver us
Strangers no more
For we have a home in You

Righteousness of Zion go forth as brightness
Salvation thereof as a lamp that burns
Show us, teach us, lead us
Strangers no more
You've opened the door
A family in unity
Grafted on Your righteous tree
And we have a home in You

# －Acknowledgements －

Regarding those who have helped me in my writing journey. . .

I simply cannot thank anyone but the Lord. Those I will be mentioning, understand this.

Thank You, Father, for Shirley. I am so grateful that the sanctification You've done in her life has benefited mine as well. I know that she labors in Your Word, and I appreciate that You've instructed me through her all these years. Therefore, I esteem her highly in love, as being over me in You. There are no words to thank you enough. As a good and faithful Shepherd, Lord, You have told me the things I needed to hear, and in receiving the love of Your truth, I can testify with full assurance that all of Your Words are right and true. I thank You for Your righteous judgments. I have witnessed them personally (through her), and am changed because of them. I will always be most grateful for this spiritual covering. (I Thess 5:12,13)

Thank You, Father, for my "fine fellow and family man." You provide and protect me so well through Adam, and I couldn't be more grateful for the work You've done in our marriage. I pray that we continue to grow closer to You and closer to each other; and that You are behind every single decision we make together (as one) and individually.

I further thank You for the financial covering that You have provided through Adam's diligence in laboring for this family. All we have ever needed, and ever will need – is enough. I praise You today, for "enough." I also praise You for being faithful to me in Your Word and promises. Adam is precious. He is one of a kind, and I thank You for him.

Thank You, Father, for Renee. The sweetest, most obedient heart any mother could want in a daughter. I am so grateful for the countless prayers that You've prayed over this family through her, the smile that can warm even the most hopeless soul, and a warmth that radiates Your love and anointing. I praise You, Lord, for the opportunity to know what it's like not only to have a daughter, but also to have a sister in the same body.

Thank You, Father, for Randy. I appreciate so much that as the Creator, You've formed him with the talent and passion for film, special effects, and computer graphics that has motivated him. It's through this talent and calling that Your song book has such a beautiful and appropriate cover. However, it is through the meek and soft answers that You've placed in Him, that I see Your gentle nature ever on display. I ask You, as I make mention of him in my prayer, that he be rewarded for his willingness to assist in this ministry, according to Your will.

Thank You, Father, for Anna. The youngest "sister" I have. It is through this child that I have felt Your encouragement the most. Whether she joyfully says, "That's my favorite song yet!" or she asks in anticipation, "Have you gotten any new songs lately?" Her constant joy and love for listening have been more support than anyone could ever hope to have. I praise You, Lord, for this peculiar treasure.

Thank You, Father, for the rest of my family. Thank You for putting in my life the family you hand-picked just for me. As I lift them up to You today, I ask You to remember the exhortations, admonitions, conviction, fellowship, and countless services that I have received due to their obedience to You. I, additionally, pray for their households, and any future spouses and generations.

I praise You, Lord, for the countless ways You manifest Yourself among these people, the ways You are able to comfort my heart, and for supporting the ministry to which You have called me. To You be all the credit, honor, and glory. In Jesus' name. Amen.

## -Reflection-

- Reflection -

## -Reflection-

- Reflection -

www.ingramcontent.com/pod-product-compliance
Lightning Source LLC
Chambersburg PA
CBHW021822090426
42811CB00032B/1984/J